AF556905

BETTY BOOP™
99
Secrets

First published in 2010 by Blue Sky Books Ltd
2nd Floor, Berkeley Square House, Berkeley Square, London W1J 6BD
www.blueskybooks.co.uk

British Cataloguing-in-Publication Data:
A catalogue record of this book is available from the British Library.

ISBN 978-1-907309-00-7

Designed by Spirit Design Consultants, London
www.spirit-design.com

Editorial contribution: Sacha Markin

Printed and bound in China through Printworks Int. Ltd.

The secret's out –
Betty Boop
shares all!

Soak away the day... relax with
your favourite bubble bath –
is-this-the-way-to-heaven?

An apple a day really does keep the Doctor away – such a pity, mine is so-o-o-o good looking!

1-2-3... close your eyes for just 30 teeny seconds and relax – did you find yourself? What do you mean, you weren't lost?

PMA – Positive Mental Attitude. Say after me: I will fit in that dress, I will fit in that dress, I will fit in that dress.

Wakey, wakey... soak a face cloth in water with a few drops of peppermint oil. Pop it in a nice cool fridge, then drape over your face for a minute or two - W-O-W W-E-E

Betty Boop's Lemon Zinger – pop a slice of lemon in some hot water and sip away – so easy, so good!

Rushing here,
rushing there,
slow down; take
a deep breath...
ahhh, that's better.

Take the day off and do nothing –
(no, you can't go shopping!)

Turn off that TV, turn off that
phone... and wave bye-bye world
– everybody needs a little P&Q
now and then.

Tiptoe round barefoot and wiggle those toes. Great for your feet (and they can't hear you coming – Sssshhh!)

Take good care of your body sweetie, it's the only one you've got – and its so-o-o-o lovely!

SUCH SWEET DREAMS – pop a few drops of lavender on your pillow and close your eyes... is it morning already?

What pretty peepers! Keep those eyes shining bright by dabbing cold milk on your eyelids first thing in the morning – lovely!

Strike a pose... yoga's very good for you and so easy to do at home – take a look at my legs!

Walking is such great exercise for those legs (and for getting where you need to go!)... off you trot.

Cool as a... cucumber, pop two slices on your eyes and relax. Was that the door? Oh, I think my stress just left.

Pat yourself head to toe in your favourite body cream – did I miss a spot?

It's crunch time – big, crispy, green salads not only taste good, they are good – d-e-l-i-c-i-o-u-s!

One of those days? Treat yourself to a new hair cut, or your nails painted – wow, the world really is a different place.

Cranberry Crush – zap some cranberry juice and ice in the blender, easy – feel good, inside and out! Can you pass me a straw please? Thank you.

Want to lose weight in an instant? Well you can start by clearing out that handbag. Cheeky!

Light a few scented candles and burn your favourite oil (lavender or rose), lie back and relax. Ahhhh, heavenly!

Breakfast is so-o-o-o important with such a busy day ahead – I never, ever miss mine – it's my golden rule. Oh, thank you, one slice!

Sip on green tea with a little lemon or honey to make it extra yummy – just like you!

Mmmm, this smells good enough to drink – cooled chamomile tea is a great rinse for those pesky little skin blemishes – ummm, that's better!

GOLDEN TIP! For silky smooth skin, body brush before every bath. Your skin will feel heavenly and extra huggable, oohhh!

Milk is very good for you. It's got lots of vitamins and can calm you in an instant – I sip mine through a straw, want to try?

Smart girls always wear sun block, whatever the weather! Keep those naughty wrinkles at bay, today, tomorrow, the day after, next week... I think they got the message Betty!

Zzzzzz – a good night's sleep really is the best beauty aid there is.

Perfect pins? Luscious lips? Whatever they are, play up your best bits! Oh, where do I start?

Eating fruit is one of my favourite pass-times – it's berry good for you! Ohhhh!

Use a soft toothbrush on those luscious lips of yours, it smoothes away that naughty dry skin and gives your lips a massage too!

Snack on the go? Carry some nuts and seeds with you for when you're out and about... ummmm delicious.

Get outta town. I'm sorry, I didn't mean to be rude. Take a walk in the country or by the sea for a quick little pick-me-up. Oh, you want me to come too?

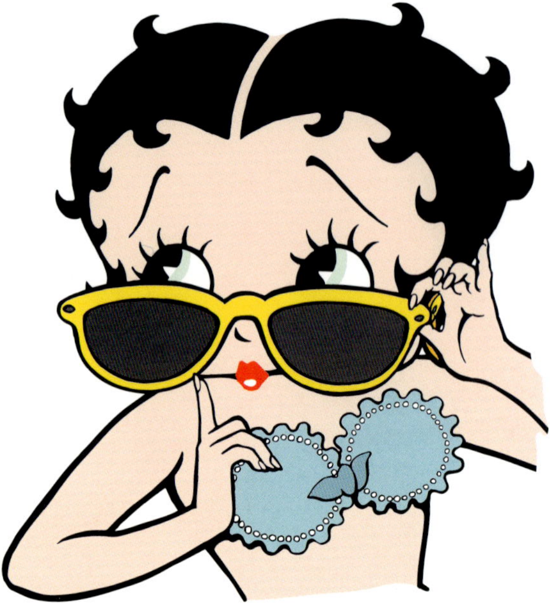

Is she a movie star? Big shades don't only look great; they protect those pretty peepers too!

Feeling a little creaky? Try a few stretches... why, I feel better already.

A, B, C, D (I thought I'd learnt my alphabet)... vitamins give you a boost and keep you looking great.

Spray a dash of your favourite scent for an instant mood lift. Pat it on your wrists, your neck, or behind your ears… feeling better? I told you so!

Chew, chew… try chewing your food a little longer. It not only tastes better, it's good for you too.

Spray your clothes and bedding with a favourite scent. Rosemary, lavender and orange blossom are my favourites – uhmmm, boop-a-licious.

Take time to look your best!

Billion Dollar Scrub – Mix up 2 handfuls of sea salt with 2 spoonfuls of your favourite massage oil, rub into your skin, then soak in a lovely warm bath – smooth and silky, what a perfect combination!

No matter how fast I run, I can never keep up with fashion... get your own style and stand out from the crowd!

Try sipping a glass of water before meals, you won't eat quite so much. Thank you, that's more than plenty.

Waste some time (you have my permission!)... it's lovely just doing nothing; try it once in a while.

Get a new haircut! Why, I hardly recognised you.

Need a wake-up call? Take
a 30 second cold shower...
oh my word!

Tootsie Treat – try a foot massage
cream with a hint of mint...
so-o-o-o soothing, so-o-o-o fresh.

49

Get out of the house... there's so much to do!

Sssshhh... silence is a lovely way to relax! Oh my, I can almost hear myself think.

Jelly is really good for keeping nails strong – it tastes good too...

Be kind to yourself. Life has its little ups and downs. I wish you more ups than downs!

Try getting up a little earlier and watching the sunrise... oh, that's so pretty!

Natural beauty is the in thing!
Try henna to colour your hair,
natural creams for your face.
Wow, you just stopped traffic!

Giggle... it's the quickest way to feel good.

All tucked up? Before you drift off,
think of something that made you
happy that day – a smile, a song, the
sunshine – oh, that handsome man
did wink at me, didn't he... ahhh!

Aqua-licious! Water is so-o-o-o good for you. Drink lots of it; it's healthy and great for your skin. Oh, a little ice and lemon would be lovely.

Think Green! Get a lovely plant for your desk. How pretty!

Forget the elevator, take the stairs once in a while...

Don't be shy... look at people when you're talking to them, it's the polite thing to do.

Give those fizzy drinks a miss, juice is so-o-o-o much nicer.

Think yourself happy! “I’m on top of the world; I’m on top of the world. No really, I’m on top of the world, can someone please help me down?” pheww, thank you!

Cut back on coffee, your body will thank you.

Closet Clearout Time – you come back here missy! "You don't fit... out with you... Oh, what was I thinking..? There you go, just my favourites!"

Talk when you're feeling blue, that's what friends are for.

Optimists live so much longer. Now, where was that bright side again?

Believe in yourself!
Boop-oop-a-doop!

Tell people you love them.
I love you! Why, thank you,
I love you too!

Don't let work rule your life... say after me: I'm sorry Boss, but I've got to go home!

Be your own best friend.

What did you say; you haven't got a thing to wear? Really? Clothes swap parties with friends are great for saving pennies and having fun! Oh, that's just my size.

Get yourself some happy friends who make you feel good – so-o-o-o sorry, no grouches allowed!

Meet someone who doesn't have a smile? Give them one of yours! Me, I've got lots and lots!

FRAGILE

Don't gossip – catching up on news is one thing, talking about people is something else.

Get there early... things always go so-o-o-o much better when we're not rushing.

GET FRUITY. So many to choose from... pears, blueberries, oranges, apples and bananas... healthy and yummy.

Hey you, slow down, you're already in tomorrow – take your time... enjoy yourself!

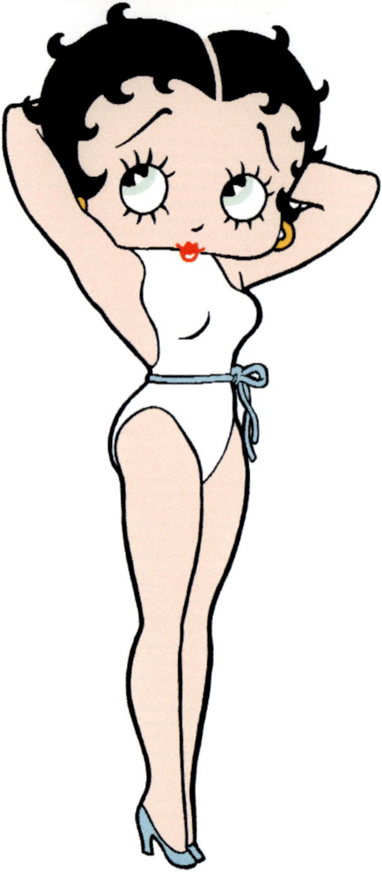

Go Girl... Yoga, Pilates, Walking, Tai Chi, they're all great for you.

Do something different – always wearing trousers? Wear a flirty skirt! Oh, you do have legs, they're nice.

Dip your tootsies in a bubbling foot spa... and float away. Come back, come back you're drifting.

Betty Boop's Herb Garden – Basil, Cumin, Fennel, Ginger, Mint, Oregano, Rosemary, Sage, Thyme... too many to mention and all so-o-o-o good for you!

Falling in love... it's the best – boop-oop-a-doop.

'Betty Boop's Summer Salad Dressing' – well, did you think I was the only dish in the kitchen? Mix a little oil, with a little lemon juice, add a touch of salt and pepper, hey presto, it's that easy.

Be nice to people, they'll feel good and you'll feel good. Can I help you with those bags, ma'am?

Beat those naughty blues... do something that makes you happy... anything at all, dance, rollerblade or sing... hey, can I come round to your place?

Powernap... Zzzzz – a few minutes sleep is great tonic. OK, what's next?

Need to calm those nerves...
take some long, deep breathes...
there, off you go!

Rise n' shine! What's the first thing I say every morning... oh, you guessed! Boop-oop-a-doop, of course!

Please sweetie, only wear clothes that fit you... so many girls don't, it's an out and out scandal!

I never ever use the D word (diet Sssshhh)... I just dropped a few pounds... ouch, they landed straight on my foot!

Fresh air! Go get some... it's right up there with kissing and holding hands!

92

Think only sunny thoughts. If those clouds come by, send them on their way... off you go!

Hey good looking, what you got cooking? Whatever it is, you can bet it's low in salt. Want a bite?

If you mean no, say no! If you mean yes, say yes! If you mean maybe, say maybe! There, I said it.

Clear out that make-up bag! Old, flaky make-up is a definite no, no. Why not clean out those flaky friends too while you're at it!

Why not get a model make-over? Wow! That really is a new you!

Mix and mingle... make some new friends. Hello, my name's Betty... Betty Boop, pleased to meet you.

A new you needs a new handbag. What's stopping you?

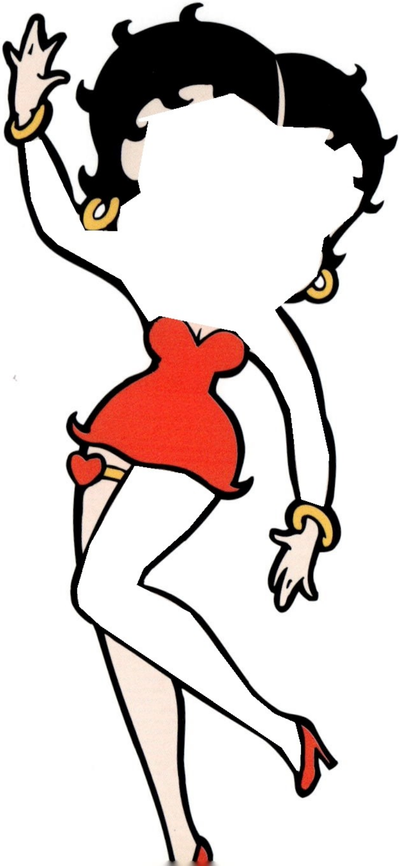

Make the most of
every day.
Boop-oop-a-doop.

Love,
Betty x

Betty Boop™

Look out for more secrets from **Betty Boop...**

Happiness

Being happy is easier than you think! Think lovely, warm, fresh towels. A cosy picnic for two. Falling in love – ahhh. Secrets to make you and everybody else happy, too!

Dating

Miss Boop's tips on looking date-great! Where should you meet on a first date? Is he Prince Charming or just another frog? Betty Boop is the expert – she's here to help you get it right!

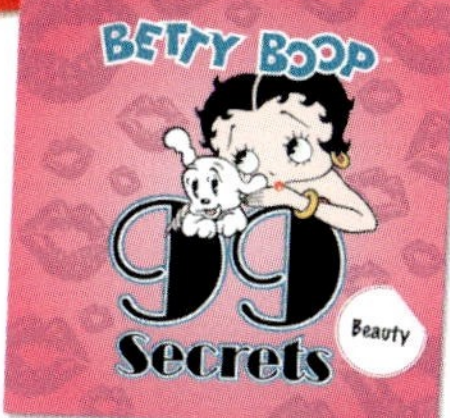

Beauty

How do you get super-luscious lashes? Boop-a-licious lips? The tan-fantastic? Read on and you'll find out.

www.bettyboop.com